SILVER BURDETT
music

AUTHORS

Elizabeth Crook, Music Consultant, State of Rhode Island
Bennett Reimer, Northwestern University, Evanston, Illinois
David S. Walker, Queens College of The City University
of New York.

SPECIAL CONTRIBUTORS

William M. Anderson (non-Western music), Aurora, Ohio
Kojo Fosu Baiden (music of Africa), Silver Springs, Maryland
Dulce B. Bohn (recorder), Wilmington, Delaware
Charles L. Boilès (music of Mexico), Bloomington, Indiana
Ian L. Bradley (Canadian music), Victoria, British Columbia, Canada
Gerald Burakoff (recorder), Levittown, New York
Henry Burnett (music of Japan), Flushing, Long Island, New York
Richard J. Colwell (testing and evaluation), Urbana, Illinois
Marilyn C. Davidson (music for Orff instruments), Bergenfield, New Jersey
Joan Davies (music of Canada and Japan), Charlottetown, P.E.I., Canada
Kay Hardesty (special education), Chautauqua, New York
James M. Harris (music in early childhood), San Francisco, California
Doris E. Hays (avant-garde music), New York City
Nazir A. Jairazbhoy (music of India), Windsor, Ontario, Canada
Maria Jordan (music of Greece), Hicksville, Long Island, New York
Robert A. Kauffman (music of Africa), Seattle, Washington
Edna Knock (music of Canada), Brandon, Manitoba, Canada
John Lidstone (visual arts), Brooklyn, New York
David McHugh (youth music), New York City
Alan P. Merriam (music of the North American Indians), Bloomington, Indiana
Lucille Mitchell (American folk songs), Alexandria, Virginia
Maria Luisa Muñoz (music of Puerto Rico), Houston, Texas

Lynn Freeman Olson (listening program), New York City
Mary E. Perrin (music in the inner city), Chicago, Illinois
Carmino Ravosa (children's song literature), Briarcliff Manor, New York
Joyce Bogusky-Reimer (avant-garde music), Wilmette, Illinois
Geraldine Slaughter (music of Africa), Washington, D.C.
Mark Slobin (music of the Near East), Middletown, Connecticut
Ruth Marie Stone (music of Africa), New York City
Leona B. Wilkins (music in the inner city), Evanston, Illinois

CONSULTANTS

Lynn Arizzi (levels 1 and 2), Reston, Virginia
Joy Browne (levels 5 and 6), Kansas City, Missouri
Nancy Crump, classroom teacher, Alexandria, Louisiana
Lyla Evans, classroom teacher, South Euclid, Ohio
Catherine Gallas, classroom teacher, Bridgeton, Missouri
Linda Haselton, classroom teacher, Westminster, California
Ruth A. Held, classroom teacher, Lancaster, Pennsylvania
Judy F. Jackson, classroom teacher, Franklin, Tennessee
Mary E. Justice, Auburn University, Auburn, Alabama
Jean Lembke (levels 3 and 4), Tonawanda, New York
Barbara Nelson, classroom teacher, Baytown, Texas
Terry Philips (youth music), New York City
Ruth Red, Director of Music Education, Houston, Texas
Mary Ann Shealy (levels 1 and 2), Florence, South Carolina
Beatrice Schattschneider (levels 1–6), Morristown, New Jersey
Paulette Schmalz, classroom teacher, Phoenix, Arizona
Sister Helen C. Schneider, Clarke College, Dubuque, Iowa
Merrill Staton (recordings), Alpine, New Jersey

SILVER BURDETT

music

ELIZABETH CROOK · BENNETT REIMER · DAVID S. WALKER

SILVER BURDETT COMPANY · MORRISTOWN, NEW JERSEY

GLENVIEW, ILLINOIS · PALO ALTO · DALLAS · ATLANTA

ACKNOWLEDGMENTS

The authors and editors of SILVER BURDETT MUSIC acknowledge with gratitude the contributions of the following persons.

Marjorie Hahn, New York
Yoriko Kozumi, Japan
Ruth Merrill, Texas
Mary Ann Nelson, Texas
Bennie Mae Oliver, Texas
Joanne Ryan, New York
Helen Spiers, Virginia
Shirley Ventrone, Rhode Island
Avonelle Walker, New York

Credit and appreciation are due publishers and copyright owners for use of the following:

"Music" from A Rocket in My Pocket compiled by Carl Withers. Copyright 1948 by Carl Withers. Reprinted by permission of Holt, Rinehart and Winston, Inc. and The Bodley Head (published in the UK by The Bodley Head).

"Thunder" by Glenys Van Every, from Miracles, collected by Richard Lewis. Copyright © 1966 by Richard Lewis. Reprinted by permission of Simon & Schuster, a Division of Gulf & Western Corporation.

CONTENTS

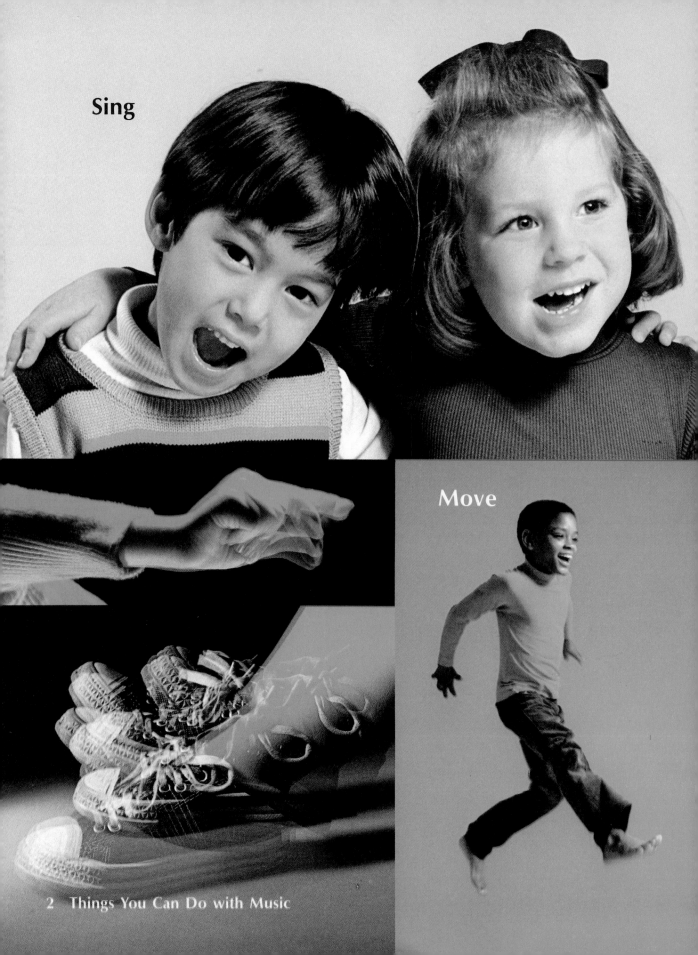

Sing

Move

Play

Listen

People, animals, and things move.

Fast

Slow

Tempo 5

Which sounds are **loud**?

Which sounds are **soft**?

Make a **long** motion.

Make a **short** motion.

FOOTPATH

Joyce Bogusky-Reimer

© 1980 Joyce Bogusky-Reimer

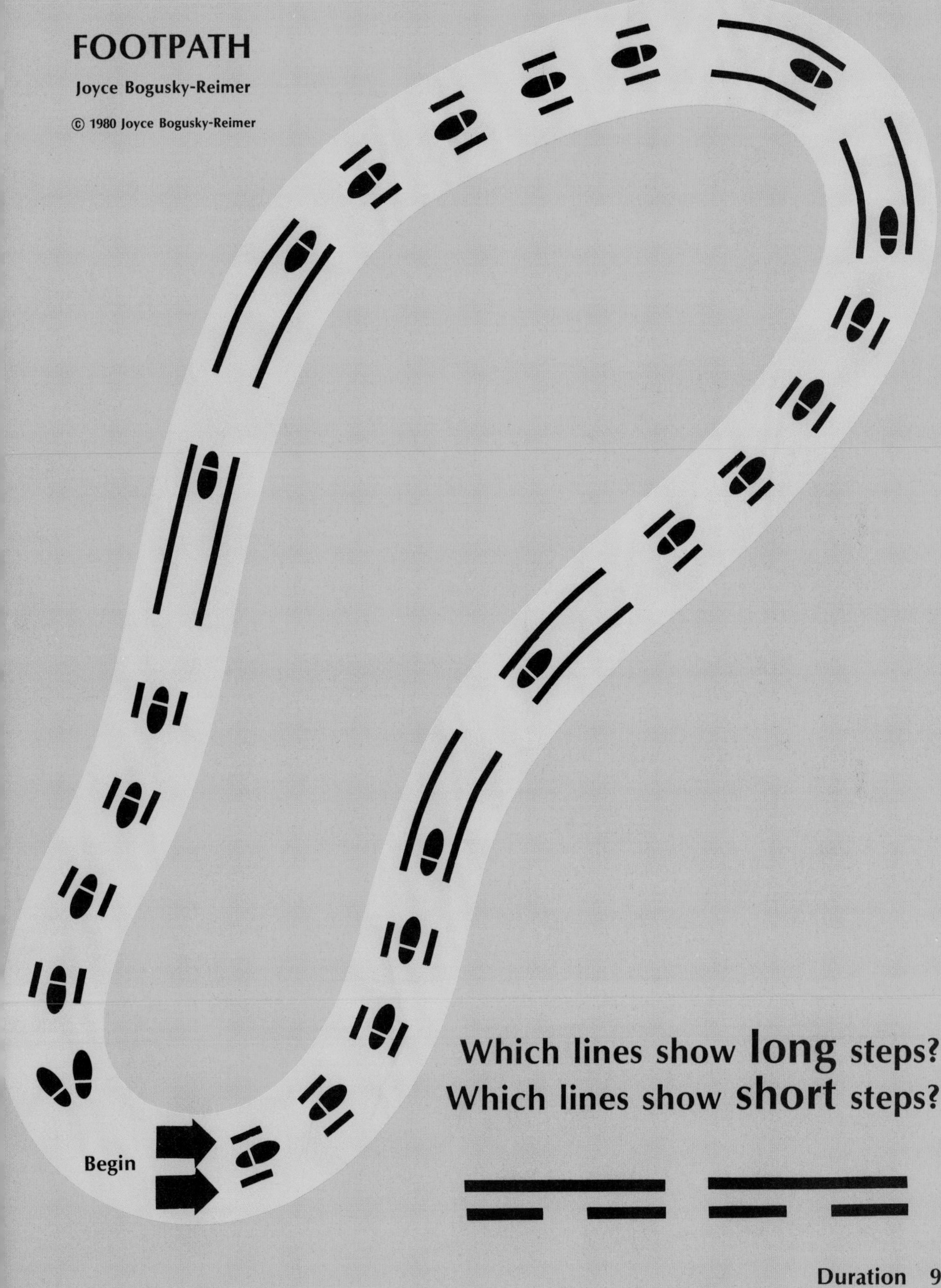

Begin

Which lines show **long** steps?
Which lines show **short** steps?

Duration 9

high

Reach **high.**

Reach **low.**

Play **high** sounds.

Play **low** sounds.

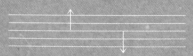

Who is playing **high** sounds?

Who is playing **low** sounds?

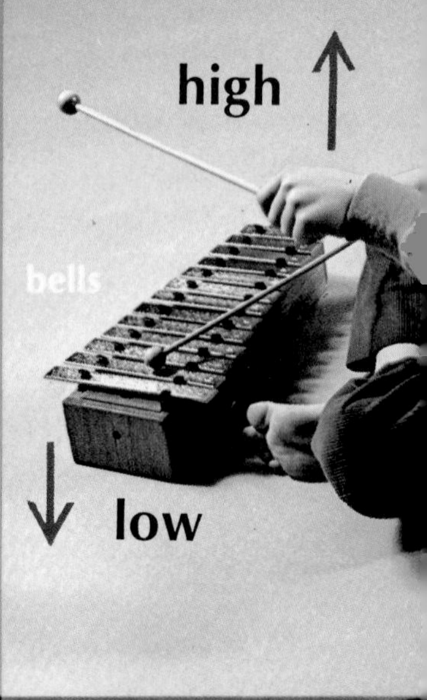

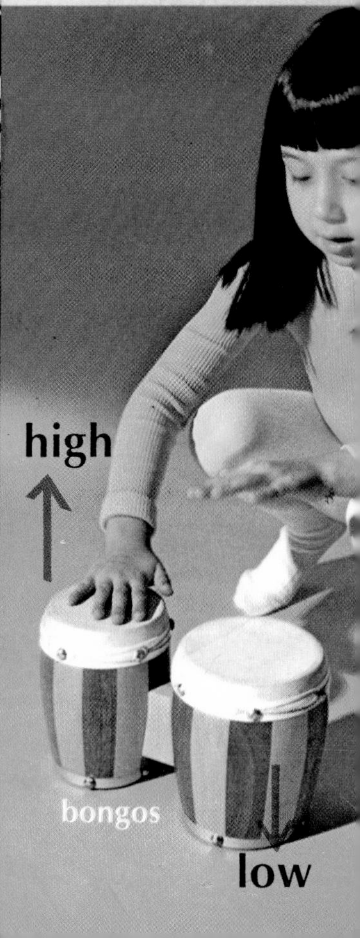

high ↑

bells

low ↓ low

high
↑
low

autoharp

high
↑

bongos

Play **high** and **low** sounds.

high C

Bells

low C

piano

What is happening
in each picture?

Match the
pictures
with the sounds
you hear.

These games use a steady beat.

Some music has a steady beat.

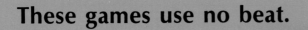

These games use no beat.

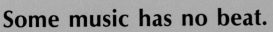

Some music has no beat.

زاید بر بای ایستاده تا چون بر زمین افتد استخوانش شکسته نشود و بیرز از شهوت اندل با بند چون آید وی کشی کند بو مینهای شرقی و ایب خوش رود بمرغزاری اندر که کل اصناح بسیار باشد و بوی می کند دومی

ومی خورد تا شهوت زیادت کردد و ماده با او باشد و از نو جوان شود و چون بکشر آید از زبان بسیار کند

The Arts: Variation 19

Play steady beats on a drum.

Play loud.

Play long sounds.

Play soft.

How are the pictures different?

How are the sounds different?

How do the shapes show what you played?

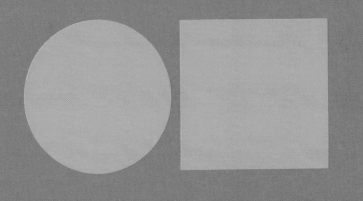

How do the letters show what you played?

You played music in AB form.

Get on board!

How do the shapes match the pictures?

How do the letters match the pictures?

"Get on Board" is in ABA form.

How are these buildings different?
How are they alike?

1. | | | | | | |

2. | | | | | | | | | | | |||||

3. | | | | | | | | | | | | | | |

Which lines show the steady beat?
Which lines show the beat getting faster?
Which lines show the beat getting slower?

Beat 31

Match the pictures with the sounds you hear.

Play steady beats on bells.

high C

maracas

man

bells

wood block

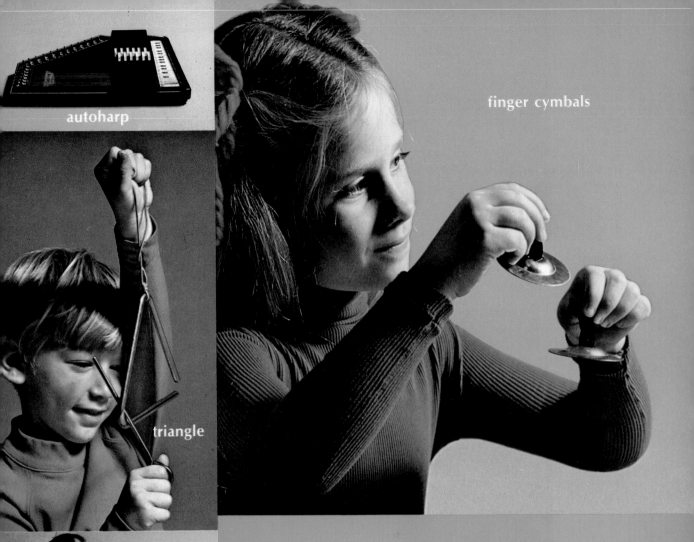

autoharp

finger cymbals

triangle

drum

Play steady beats on a drum.

flute

guitar

drums

trumpet

**Match the pictures with
the sounds you hear.**

violin

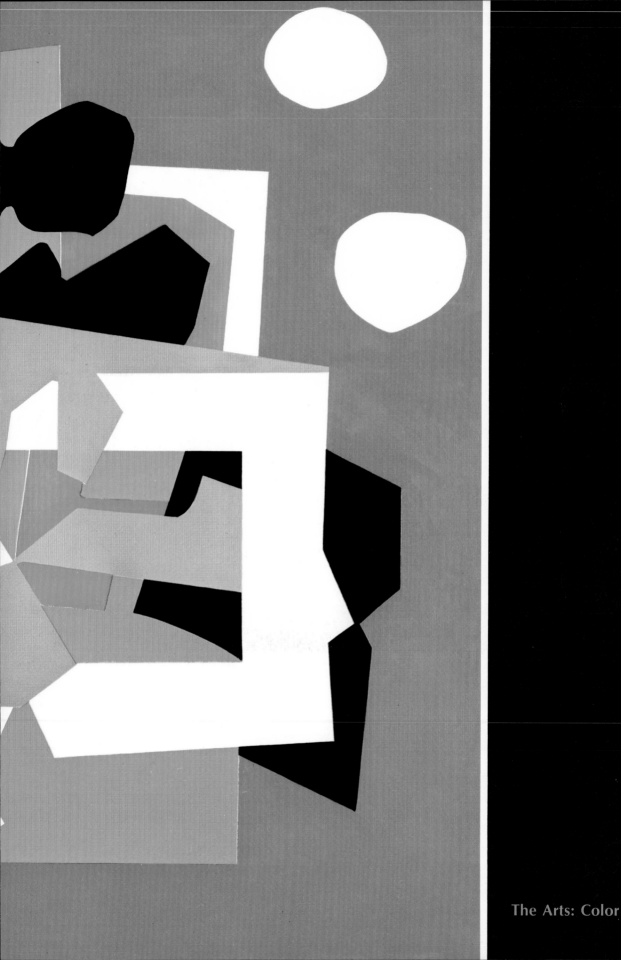

The Arts: Color

Which child is pointed out in each row?

This mark is an accent. >
It can point out, or stress, beats.
Which beat has an accent in each row?
Show the accents with your voice.

1.
I HEAR the drummer strike the sky.

2. 
I hear the DRUMMER strike the sky.

3.
I hear the drummer STRIKE the sky.

4.
I hear the drummer strike the SKY.

How does the picture show sets of two?

How does the picture show sets of three?

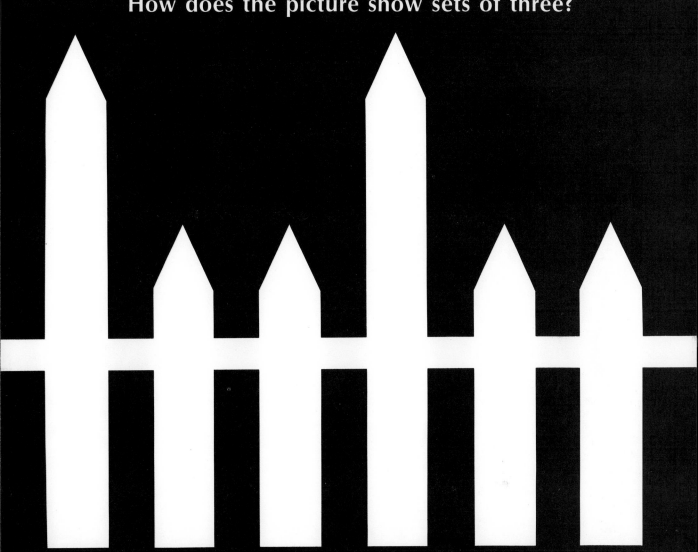

upward

Ev - 'ry - bod - y wants to sing!

crick - et's song

downward

**upward
and
downward**

Hal-le-lu - jah!

Play downward sounds on the bells.

THE CRICKET'S SONG

Folk Song from the Ukraine   English Words by Leo R. Israel

F♯   E   D

Ev'rything is silent but the crick-et's song,

But the cricket's, but the cricket's, but the crick-et's song.

While the rest are busy he sings all day long,

Singing all day, singing all day, singing all day long.

Play sounds that move upward and downward.

THAT IS WHAT HE SAY

American Folk Song

"TELL ME WHAT THE JAYBIRD SAY," MELODY AND WORDS FROM RECORD No. 4057. AFS. LIBRARY OF CONGRESS.

1. Jay bird say,   "Jay,   jay,   jay,"

2. Mockingbird say, "Whee, dee,   dee,"

3. Chee dee say,   "Chee, dee,   dee,"

C D E D C
That is what he say.

4. Old crow say,   "Crah, crah, crah,"

5. Old hawk say,   "Chick, chick, chick,"

6. Partridge say,   "Bob,   bob, white,"

7. Old owl say,   "Whoo, whoo, whoo,"

Here are endings of songs you know.
Find one that moves upward. Downward.
Find one that moves upward and downward.

1. Ev - 'ry - bod - y wants to sing!

2. Smashed to piec - es   on   the ground.

3. buy mo - las - ses can - dy.

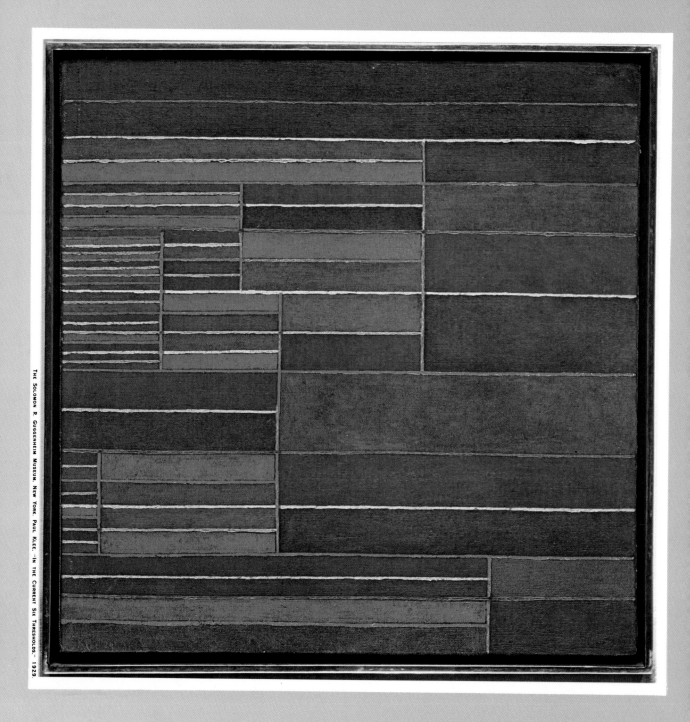

What lines do you see in this painting?

What lines do you see
in this building?

Clap these patterns of long and short sounds.

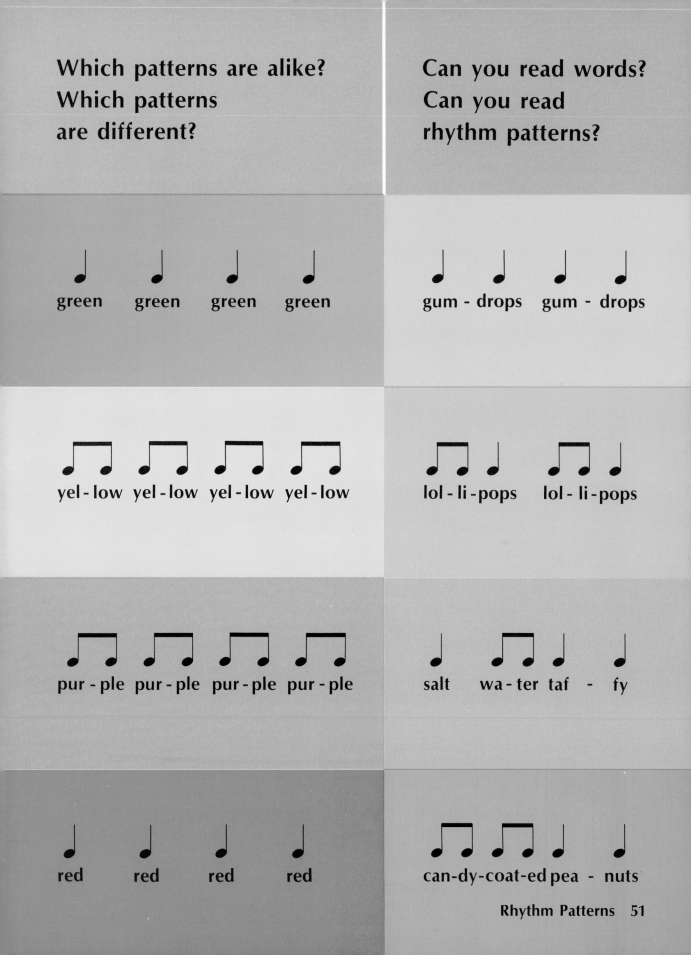

Which patterns are alike?
Which patterns are different?

green   green   green   green

yel-low yel-low yel-low yel-low

pur-ple pur-ple pur-ple pur-ple

red   red   red   red

Can you read words?
Can you read rhythm patterns?

gum - drops gum - drops

lol - li -pops lol - li -pops

salt   wa - ter taf - fy

can-dy-coat-ed pea - nuts

Rhythm Patterns 51

Read rhythm patterns in songs.

GREAT BIG STARS

Black Spiritual

♪ ♪ ♩

Great big stars 'way up yonder,

♪ ♪ ♩

Great big stars 'way up yonder,

♪ ♪ ♩

Great big stars 'way up yonder,

♩ ♩

Oh, my little soul's gonna shine, shine!

♩ ♩

Oh, my little soul's gonna shine, shine!

SKIP TO MY LOU

American Game Song

Flies in the buttermilk, shoo, fly, shoo!   (Sing 3 times.)

Skip to my Lou, my dar - ling.

CANDY STORE

Marilyn Copeland Davidson

What shall we buy   at the can - dy   store? They have

gum - drops,   lol - li-pops,   lem-on drops, and more!

Can-dy-coat-ed pea - nuts   that you can't ig-nore,

Salt   wa-ter taf - fy!   We've tried that be-fore!

Choose what you want.   I'll   meet you at the door!

Rhythm Patterns   53

Find the short phrases. Find the long phrase.

MUSIC

There's music in a hammer,

There's music in a nail,

There's music in a pussy cat when you step upon her tail.

Carl Withers

Listen for short phrases. Listen for long phrases.

OLD JOE

Folk Song from Texas

FROM THE SMALL SINGER BY ROBERTA MCLAUGHLIN AND LUCILLE WOOD: COPYRIGHT 1969 BY BOWMAR/NOBLE PUBLISHERS, INC. USED BY PERMISSION OF PUBLISHER.

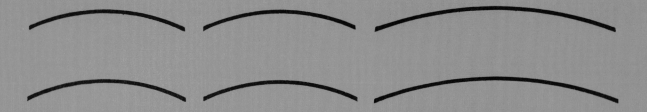

Whoa, Joe!

Follow the phrases in this music.

THE MOON IS COMING OUT

Children's Song from Japan   English Words by Kazuo Akiyama

FROM CHILDREN'S SONGS FROM JAPAN. © COPYRIGHT: EDWARD B. MARKS MUSIC CORPORATION. USED BY PERMISSION.

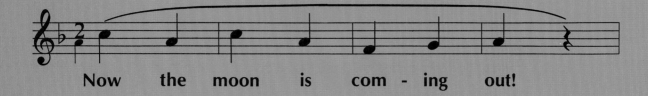

Now   the   moon   is   com - ing   out!

Big and round, so big and round, as round___ as a tray.

Moon is big and round, just   like   a   tray.

Sing the ending note.

Play the ending note.

THE FLEA AND THE MOUSE

Folk Song from Spain   English Words by Jacqueline Froom

MELODY, "LA PULGA Y EL PIOJO," REPRINTED FROM CANCIONERO POPULAR DE LA PROVINCIA DE MADRID (1951) BY PERMISSION OF
THE INSTITUTO ESPAÑOL DE MUSICOLOGIA, BARCELONA. LYRICS, "MARRIAGE," REPRINTED FROM
CHILDREN'S SONGS OF SPAIN BY PERMISSION OF THE PUBLISHERS, OXFORD UNIVERSITY PRESS, LONDON.

1.   There was once a flea

who loved a pretty mouse.

But they could not marry

for they had no

Fiddle dee, fiddle doh, fiddle

2.   There was once a pig

who loved a pretty snake.

But they could not marry

for they had no

Fiddle dee, fiddle doh, fiddle

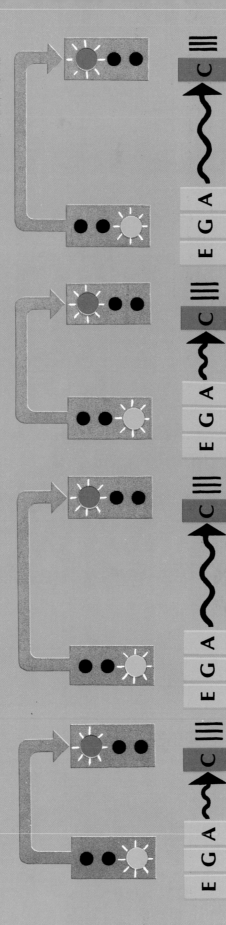

STREET MUSIC

Joyce Bogusky-Reimer

1502

Sing a melody alone.

1.

Now add harmony.

2.

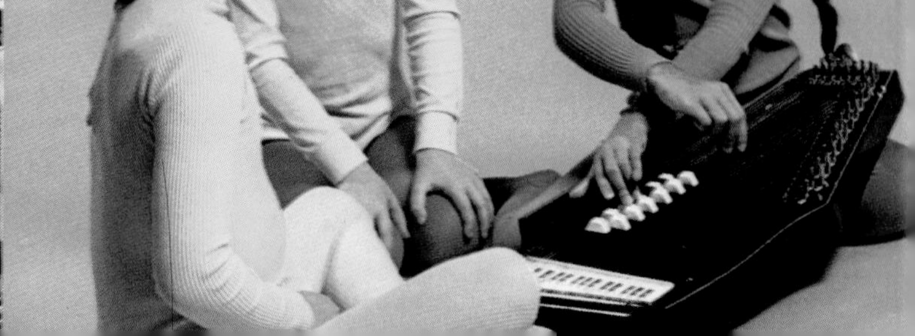

Add harmony to songs you know.

Who I Am

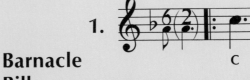

Barnacle Bill

Clap Your Hands

Never Sleep Late Any More

I'm Gonna Sing

How are the girls' clothes alike?
How are they different?
How are the boys' clothes alike?
How are they different?

Which bell part shows repeated tones?
Which one shows tones moving by step?
Which one shows leaps from high to low?

Play one of the parts with "Ringing Bells."

What can you do with music?

RINGING BELLS

Folk Song from Germany   **English Words by Trudi Eichenlaub**

FROM SING MIT. SONGBOOK FOR LOWER GRADES OF PUBLIC SCHOOLS. PUBLISHER: R. OLDENBOURG, MUNICH 1964. REPRINTED BY PERMISSION.

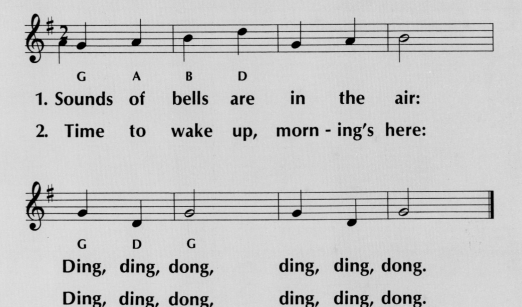

G   A   B   D

1. Sounds of   bells are   in   the   air:
2. Time   to   wake up, morn - ing's here:

G   D   G

Ding, ding, dong,   ding, ding, dong.
Ding, ding, dong,   ding, ding, dong.

Use what you know. Play this song on bells.

JEREMIAH, BLOW THE FIRE

Traditional

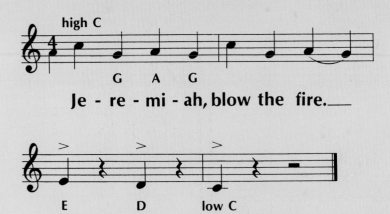

high C

G   A   G

Je - re - mi - ah, blow the fire.___

E   D   low C

Puff!   Puff!   Puff!

Intervals 65

What do you think will be in the mystery box?

1	2	3	4	5	6	7	?
C	D	E	F	G	A	B	?

Play this row of sounds on bells.

Does it sound finished at the end?

F B D C G A E

1.

2.

PICTURE CREDITS

3 4 5 6 7 8 9 10—RRD—88 87 86 85 84 83 82